I0621036

SPEND A DAY WITH

Dr. Ralph "Defender" Morales

-creative-resilient-curious-talented-

Copyright © 2025

All Rights Reserved

No part of this book may be reproduced or transmitted in any form or by any means, electronic or mechanical, including photocopying, recording, or by any information storage and retrieval system without the written permission of the author, except where permitted by law.

To my beloved son, Alexander (Alex), and to all the wonderful children on their unique journeys: we see you, we hear you, and we celebrate the beauty of who you are. We are here for you, always.

Acknowledgment

A heartfelt gratitude to all the teachers, educators, and therapists who have stood by Alex and countless others since day one. Your unwavering support and dedication have provided hope for a brighter future, even when challenges seemed insurmountable. Your guidance has helped Alex and many others in similar journeys to achieve more than they ever imagined.

Thank you to all the ABA therapists and speech therapists around the world for your invaluable contributions.

Author's Note

As a father devoted to my remarkable child, my journey has been one of seeking answers to help him achieve what once felt impossible. Together, we unlock closed doors, tirelessly working to reach his fullest potential.

There's no one-size-fits-all playbook for raising a child with autism. It's a path that invites us to embrace their unique journey, allowing them to discover who they are while offering unwavering support and consistent, unconditional love. In this endeavor, we can break stereotypes, celebrate milestones, and honor each achievement as a grand occasion.

Let us unite as their loudest advocates, championing these creative, talented children and cheering them on every step of the way. Together, we can illuminate the way forward, fostering a world that embraces their extraordinary gifts.

Hi, my name is Alex.
I don't say much,
but I know what I like!
Come spend the
day with me,
and you will see.

I enjoy going to the farm. It's my happy place.
I get to see and feed the animals on the farm.

I may not say much, but it shows
I am happy with giggles and a big smile.

I like to go to the pool.
I get to slide and swim freely.

I may not say much, but it shows I'm having a blast with a big splash.
"Watch out!"

I like to go to the playground. It's where I can express my emotions—happily and freely—through my shouts of excitement, stimming, or simply by swinging and sliding some more, just be myself.

"Weeee, look at meeee,"
as I reach for the sky.

I may not say much,
but it shows my playful
side as I joyfully shout with a
burst of excitement,

I like to ride the bus to school. It helps me to be independent and brave to do things on my own.

I may not say much, but it shows
I'm courageous when I stomp
my happy feet and shout,
"Here comes the bus!"

I like to go to school.
It is where I get to
learn my numbers,
ABCs and
social interactions.

I may not say much, but it shows
I am alert as I sing, share, and try to speak.
Most times, I just repeat.

I like to fly on airplanes.
It allows me to see my world differently from above,
along with other places around the world.

I may not say much, but It shows
I'm an adventurous explorer as I point towards the window
with excitement! Wow, look at the sky, are we there yet!?

I like to go out to eat. I always order the same thing-crispy, crunchy chicken nuggets.

I may not say much, but it shows
I enjoy every delicious bite with the
loud munch sounds of crunches.
"Crunch, crunch, crunch!"

But there are also places where I must go, like the hospital. However, The medical staff always goes above and beyond to ensure I get the best care I need, and I appreciate that!

I may not say much,
but it shows I am thankful
with a thumbs up and
a happy grin.

To include visits to the dentist. I may not say much, but I am happy to share my freshly cleaned SUPER-sparkling smile with the world and even more thankful!

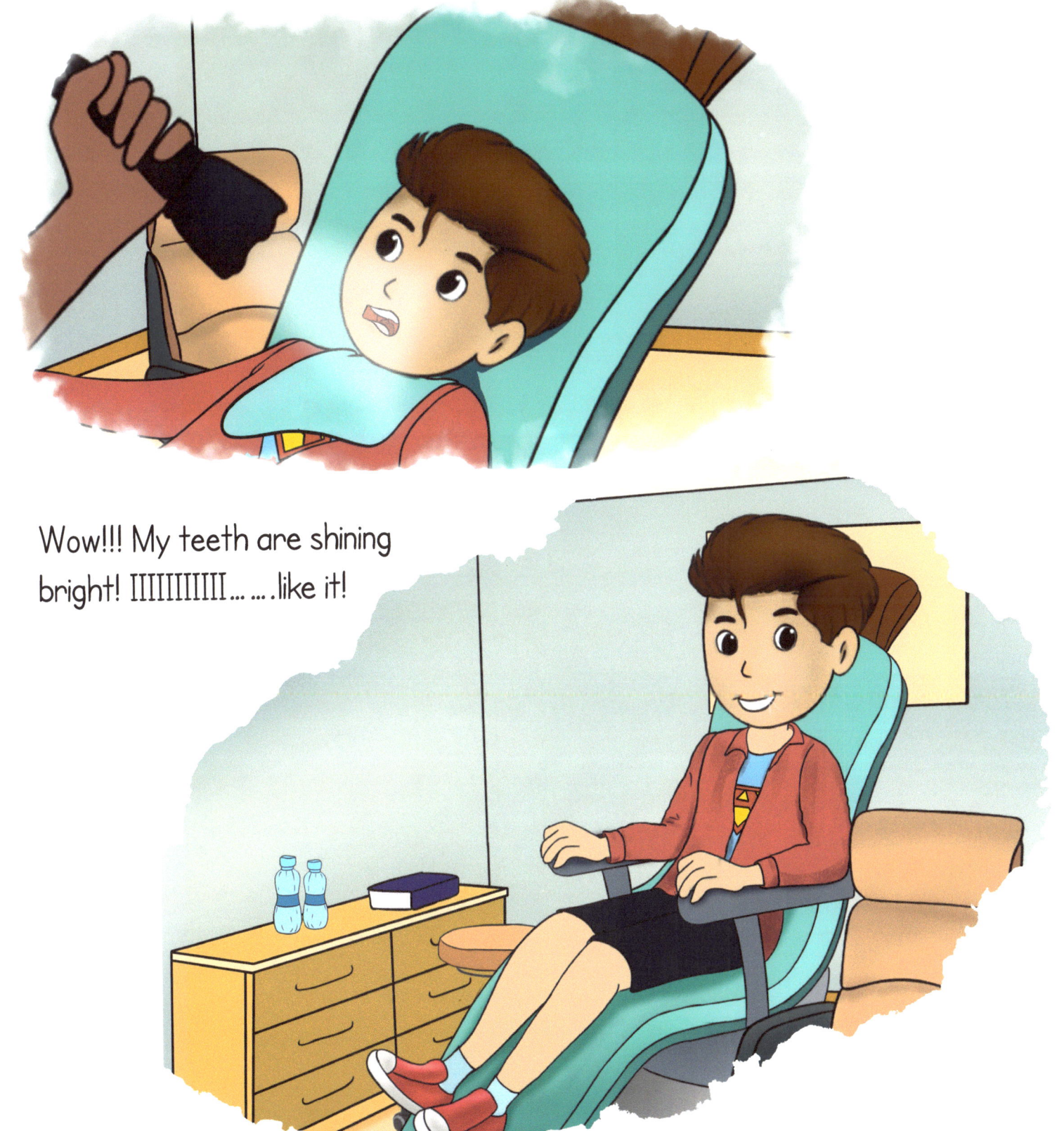

Wow!!! My teeth are shining bright! IIIIIIIIII... ....like it!

"welcor
baaaaa

Another place where I must go is the bathroom.
It's where I do my "doo" number one and two.

I may not say much,
but it shows
I have to go to
the bathroom when
I start to do my
"potty time" dance.

Going to the bathroom isn't so bad
after all! I get to enjoy my daily bath,
filled with all my favorite toys and
lots of bubbly bubbles.
It's such a great way to relax
and enjoy some more playtime!
It's like a little adventure every day!

I may not say much,
but it shows I like to play with
water as I shout with excitement,
"Splash, splash, splash!"

Well, it's getting late—thanks for spending the day with me! Now it's time to snuggle up and head to bed.

I might not always say much, but it really shows how much I enjoy sharing my world with you! And guess what? I bet we have way more in common than we might realize!

So get some rest... Because with a heroic leap, I'm off to sleep!

Good night, my friends.
Nighty night... Until our next adventure

DARE TO LEARN MORE?
Alex encourages you to soar higher and explore
THE FOLLOWING CLINICAL TERMS:

Autism

Autism Spectrum Disorder

Stimming

Perseverate

Echolalia

Manding

ABA-Applied Behavior Analysis

OT-Occupational Therapy

PT-Physical Therapy

Early Intervention

Sensory Integration

Positive Behavior Reinforcers

ALEX WILL RETURN IN

ALEX, HIS FAMILY AND YOURS

Together We Can!

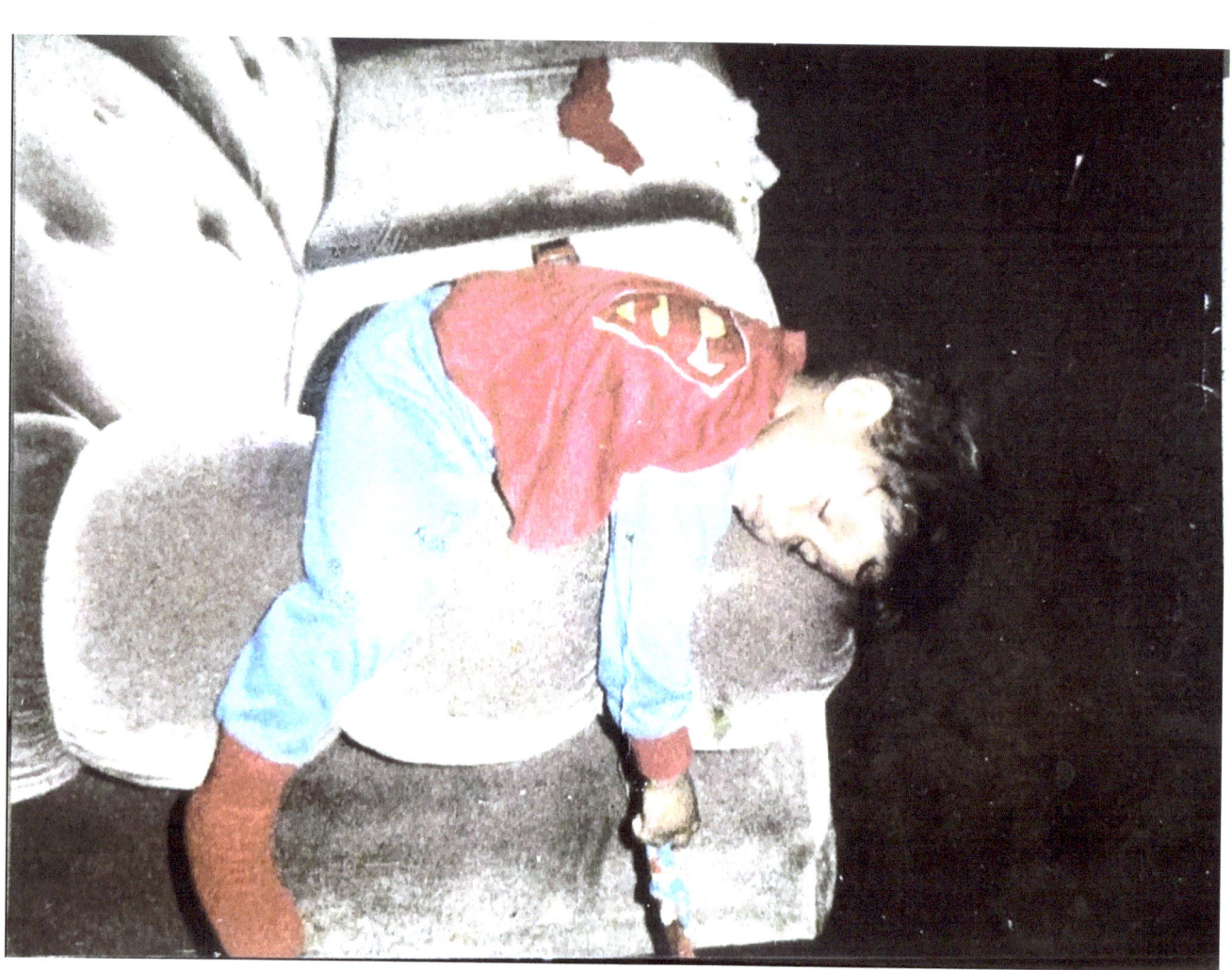

PASSING THE CAPE

As a boy, I dreamed of being as strong
as the Man of Steel.
Now, I pass down my cape to my son—
a boy who is creative, resilient,
curious, and talented.
Alex's story shows us that every child—
autistic or neurotypical—
shares the same dreams, the same joys,
and the same beautiful heart.
His journey reminds the world
that true strength isn't found in powers.
It's found in love, in family, in acceptance,
and in hope for autism acceptance.

~ Dr. Ralph *"Defender"* Morales
A.K.A.
~ **Dr. MO.**

www.ingramcontent.com/pod-product-compliance
Lightning Source LLC
Chambersburg PA
CBHW041439120626
46547CB00002B/272